RUSSELL LEE'S FSA PHOTOGRAPHS

RUSSELL LEE'S FSA PHOTOGRAPHS
of Chamisal and Peñasco
New Mexico

edited by William Wroth

Ancient City Press ● Santa Fe, New Mexico and
Taylor Museum of the Colorado Springs Fine Arts Center
Colorado Springs, Colorado

This publication was partially funded by a grant from the National Endowment for the Arts, a federal agency.

International Standard Book Number:
0–941270–24–6 Clothbound
0–941270–23–8 Paperbound
Library of Congress Catalogue Number:
85–071305

First Edition

Designed by Mary Powell

Typesetting by Business Graphics, Inc.
Albuquerque, New Mexico
Printed in the United States of America

To the people of Chamisal and Peñasco:
May they prosper.

CONTENTS

ACKNOWLEDGMENTS

The authors and the editor wish to thank Russell Lee for his interest in and support of this project since its inception in 1979. Our thanks also go to a number of Chamisal and Peñasco residents for kindly helping us identify many of the subjects in the photographs and for providing information about life in these villages in 1940.

Leroy Bellamy and Jerry Kearns of the Prints and Photographs Division of the Library of Congress have been extremely cooperative in assisting the editor with his research and coordinating the reproduction of the Lee photographs. James C. Anderson and David G. Horvath of the University of Louisville Photographic Archives provided access to the Roy Stryker Papers in their care.

Marta Weigle served as editorial consultant for the project. Her acute comments have improved all of the essays in this volume.

Custom prints were made for reproduction in this volume by the Photoduplication Service of the Library of Congress. Myron Wood and Beverly Conley very skillfully spotted the photographic prints in preparation for publication.

Many staff members of the Colorado Springs Fine Arts Center have contributed to this project. In particular, we wish to thank Jonathan Batkin for assisting with photograph selection and with publication agreements and Kelly Smith for typing and retyping the manuscript.

Mary Powell of Ancient City Press designed the book and saw it through press. Its publication was made possible by the National Endowment for the Arts, the Taylor Museum of the Colorado Springs Fine Arts Center, and Ancient City Press.

CONTRIBUTORS:

William Wroth, former curator of the Taylor Museum, is a writer and lecturer on the Southwest.

Charles L. Briggs is an anthropologist who teaches at Vassar College.

Alan M. Fern is director of the National Portrait Gallery.

INTRODUCTION

The Farm Security Administration (FSA) was one of many federal programs which were part of the New Deal response to depressed conditions in American life between 1933 and 1943. First called the Resettlement Administration when it was established by Executive Order in 1935, the FSA was to implement solutions to the crises faced by American farmers in the aftermath of drought and depression. While much of its work was devoted to studying and aiding indigent small farmers and farm laborers, one FSA division embarked upon an imaginative documentation project which today provides an invaluable record of rural America in the 1930s and early 1940s. The Historical Section of the FSA, headed by Roy E. Stryker, set out to document through photographs the conditions of rural (and later, urban) life all over the country. At various times between 1935 and 1943, Stryker's staff included, among other photographers: Walker Evans, Dorothea Lange, Arthur Rothstein, Ben Shahn, Carl Mydans, Marion Post Wolcott, John Collier, Jr., Jack Delano, John Vachon, Gordon Parks, and Russell Lee.

Lee was employed by the FSA between 1936 and 1942. He travelled across the Midwest and West from Michigan to California, recording on film what he saw in rural areas. Lee made a preliminary visit to New Mexico in 1939 and returned for a lengthy stay in the spring of 1940. In July of that year, he spent about two weeks in the neighboring Taos County mountain villages of Chamisal and Peñasco, photographing the Spanish-speaking residents and all aspects of their life.

In these and other northern New Mexico villages, Lee found a way of life that was very different from the rest of the country. In most areas, he and other FSA photographers were recording a desperate situation—the tragic upheavals and disintegration of rural life brought about by the Depression. Their purpose was frankly propagandistic: to make complacent Americans aware of the plight of the less fortunate. However, after 1938, Roy Stryker wanted his photographers to record not only those people in utter poverty but the full range of rural life in America. Thus, in New Mexico Lee did not impose a preconceived view based on the national situation. Instead he sensed and vividly recorded the still-coherent Hispanic culture he found in the villages, producing photographs showing the strength of traditional values which still informed the life of the community.

Although he had little experience with the Hispanic people of New Mexico, Lee's sensitive photographic skills enabled him to record with perfection their essential human qualities. His photographs transcend the documentary purposes for which they were made. As Alan M. Fern and William Wroth note in their concluding essay, his work appears effortless; Lee as photographer seems to be invisible. In these qualities he approaches the criteria for greatness, for great art must come without effort and without the conscious imposition of the artist's individuality. The true artist works without self interest, providing a channel for the expression of work that is far greater than he.

Lee's work in Chamisal and Peñasco was intended as a thorough, in-depth documentation of traditional Hispanic communities in northern New Mexico. The photographs he made there constitute an important visual document of a way of life that was and still is little known and appreciated by the larger society. The two villages were carefully chosen following a preliminary trip to Taos County in 1939 and after much research and consultation with New Mexican scholars and authorities in 1940. Lee and Stryker had hoped to publish the "Spanish-American story" exemplified in these remote communities as a picture book with interpretive text that would make it better known to the American public. At the time, they were not able to accomplish this goal, which today remains a valid one. It is the continued need for such a publication and the high quality of Lee's photographic work which has prompted the editing of the present book.

To date, the only published, in-depth photographic essay of New Mexican village life in the 1930s and early 1940s is *A Camera Report on El Cerrito*, by Irving Rusinow.[1] Few other photographs have been published, although many were taken in the rather extensive empirical documentation projects undertaken in northern New Mexico by the FSA and other agencies within the United States Department of Agriculture, notably the Soil Conservation Service.[2] Most of these reports were simply mimeographed, if published at all, and the accompanying photographs by Lee, Rusinow, and others languished in agency files along with all the other verbal and visual documents of traditional Hispanic life.

Almost all the photographs in this collection are published here for the first time. Viewing them, we may learn something of the particulars of Hispanic village life as it existed forty-five years ago. It is a way of life in which to this day values and practices brought during the colonial period from Mexico and ultimately from Spain have been preserved.

We perceive immediately the close relation of the people to their land, their natural skill and delight in handicrafts such as the construction of adobe homes, and their participation in the round of domestic and community activities. While such details of particular practices are always fascinating to a viewer outside the culture, of greater importance in Lee's photographs are the striking human qualities of the subjects. We see them not as statistics for relief rolls or as stereotypic poverty cases but as strong, often joyful human beings carrying out their daily tasks. They are seemingly unconcerned that a "great depression" has traumatized the rest of the nation for the past decade. As Charles L. Briggs notes in his essay, "Remembering the Past," the residents of Chamisal today look back upon the 1930s not as a disastrous period but as one in which traditional cooperative, communal values still structured village life.

Lee's photographs record Hispanic village life on the eve of the most decisive change in its history: the beginning of World War II. The loss of community so eloquently lamented by Briggs's informants began with changes provoked by the traumatic effects of that war on every aspect of village life. Prior to World War II, in spite of near-crisis pressures, communal values still ordered life in the villages, and they are expressed in the everyday tasks which Lee documents: fishing, adobe construction, domestic work, and other forms of hand crafts.

These values are also expressed in the *quality* of life. In Chamisal and Peñasco, as Charles L. Briggs shows, the quality of life involves a sense of cooperation, a respect for the land, and the desire for independence. The achievement of these ends and hence the marks of success in life are the result first of adherence to God's will and second of the cultivation of the human virtues which flow naturally from this adherence. Thus a person is judged not by his cleverness in accumulating wealth but by his virtues— strength and nobility of character, industriousness, respect and generosity. The man who has attained power and wealth without these qualities may be feared, but in human terms he is not respected. A saying from the Bible one often hears repeated in the villages aptly sums up this point of view: "For what is a man profited, if he shall gain the whole world, and lose his own soul?" (*Matthew 16:* 26)

In Russell Lee's sensitive portrayals of the people of Chamisal and Peñasco, we see men and women who have these priorities in order. They are concerned with the quality of human life in a real and full sense, not simply with the accumulation of power and possessions.

NOTES

1. Irving Rusinow, *A Camera Report on El Cerrito: A Typical Spanish-American Community in New Mexico*, USDA, Bureau of Agricultural Economics, Misc. Pub. No. 479 (Washington, D.C.: Government Printing Office, 1942). For a history of the BAE and subsequent studies of the now-deserted community see Richard L. Nostrand, "El Cerrito Revisited," *New Mexico Historical Review* 57 (1982): 109–22. Rusinow also contributed photographs to J. T. Reid, *It Happened in Taos* (Albuquerque: University of New Mexico Press, 1946). A few documentary photographs of Hispanic rural life were included in *New Mexico: A Guide to the Colorful State* (New York: Hastings House, 1940), produced as part of the Federal Writers' Project (later Writers' Program) of the WPA in New Mexico.

2. Many of these materials are listed in Lyle Saunders, *A Guide to Materials Bearing on Cultural Relations in New Mexico* (Albuquerque: University of New Mexico Press, 1944), and in the bibliography in part II of Marta Weigle, ed., *Hispanic Villages of Northern New Mexico: A Reprint of Volume II of The 1935 Tewa Basin Study, with Supplementary Materials* (Santa Fe: The Lightning Tree, Jene Lyon, Publisher, 1975). Additional photographs, materials, and references will be found in Marta Weigle, ed., *New Mexicans in Cameo and Camera: New Deal Documentation of Twentieth-Century Lives* (Albuquerque: University of New Mexico Press, forthcoming, fall 1985).

REMEMBERING THE PAST:
CHAMISAL AND PEÑASCO IN 1940
Charles L. Briggs

Chamisal and Peñasco were rapidly changing communities in crisis when Russell Lee visited and photographed the villagers and their way of life in 1940. Land loss and steadily increasing dependence on a cash economy had exacted a heavy toll on the area's traditional pastoral and agricultural self-sufficiency. Drought and the Depression left these villages further impoverished, with few tangible resources for subsistence.

Nevertheless, when I interviewed older residents of both communities in 1981, not everyone agreed that "those were very, very hard times." One elderly man from Chamisal told me:

The Depression hardly hit here at all. We had 4000 pounds of wheat, we had pigs, fat cows, beans. We didn't have any money, but why did we need money? We still could graze some animals in the forest. It must have been hard in the big cities, but it wasn't here. We had a lot to eat, you see. And then we had sheep and we made wool mattresses, blankets to keep us warm, pants, socks of wool. There was lots of snow, but we had lots of firewood and lots of meat inside. There weren't any jobs at all. But if somebody was broke, the people helped him. Someone brought beans, a half sack of potatoes, some flour. There were some that suffered, but we didn't suffer. Some only had a very little land, so they didn't have any way to get by.

He too recalled that life then had not been at all easy, but what he wanted me to understand was that the people still enjoyed intangible assets such as cooperation and compassion, both much more valuable than money. It is this way of life, remembered nostalgically, which contemporary residents of Chamisal and Peñasco continue to cherish and to compare, often unfavorably, with their lives today.

Both Chamisal and Peñasco were settled during the late 1700s as offshoots of nearby settlements.[1] Most of the land surrounding the communities and stretching up into the adjacent Sangre de Cristo Mountains was conveyed to the colonists through several royal Spanish grants, including the Santo Tomás Apóstol del Río de las Trampas, the Sebastián Martín, the Rancho del Río Grande, the Santa Bárbara and the Cristóbal de la Serna. Chamisal and Peñasco themselves are located on the Picurís Pueblo Grant, and encroachment by *Mexicanos* (Hispanic New Mexicans) on Picurís lands was a frequent source of friction between Hispanic and Native American neighbors.

Because of the way they utilized their resources, the villages were able to survive in a precarious natural environment. Individuals owned garden plots and house lots. Large sections of the grants were set aside as common lands for grazing livestock, hunting, obtaining timber and firewood, and the like.[2] Settlers thus were able to supplement limited agricultural produce with goat and sheep husbandry and derive a livelihood from the semiarid land. This independent, rigorous existence of 150 years' duration was coming to an end by the time of Russell Lee's visit.

The American conquest of 1846 and the subsequent influx of Anglo-Americans competing for resources generated serious pressures on native residents. Former Mexican citizens' property rights were formally guaranteed by the Treaty of Guadalupe Hidalgo in 1848,[3] but differences between Spanish and Anglo-American land laws enabled unscrupulous land speculators and the United States government to gain control of nearly all land which was not actually occupied.[4] Most of the land surrounding Chamisal and Peñasco eventually came under the control of the U.S. Forest Service and the Bureau of Land Management.[5] Such legal machinations had little impact on local residents until the 1920s, when commercial operators and government agencies began to restrict their access to vital grazing, fuelwood, and hunting lands. The inhabitants of Peñasco, Chamisal and nearby communities soon foresaw the destruction of their way of life.[6]

Mercantile and then industrial capitalism became increasingly dominant in the late nineteenth and twentieth centuries. Cash needs were exacerbated by the imposition of land taxes, absent under Spanish rule (1598–1821).[7] Families generated little cash income because they consumed most of their meat, crops, and other products themselves. Many persons thus lost even more of their land for nonpayment of taxes and/or merchants' bills.

The demise of the family herd of sheep, cattle and especially goats was critically important. Meat, goatsmilk and cheese were always crucial supplements to agricultural products. Pressure from commercial sheep and cattle ranchers and government efforts to curtail soil erosion led to a steady diminution in the number of livestock permits available to local residents for use on Forest Service and Bureau of Land Management lands. Goats were wholly excluded from the National Forest after 1958.[8] Ironically, undermining the pastoral sector of the economy devastated the agricultural part as well; the fields had been fertilized by corraling the livestock there each winter.

As a result, large numbers of men from Peñasco, Chamisal, and numerous other Mexicano communities in northern New Mexico were forced to seek migratory wage-labor employment outside the area. They worked in mines and fought fires throughout the Southwest, harvested crops in Colorado, laid and maintained track in various states, herded sheep in Wyoming and Utah, and pursued other employment. Prior to the Depression an estimated seven to ten thousand workers from the Middle Rio Grande Valley villages (land drained by the Rio Grande between Elephant Butte to the south and the New Mexico-Colorado border to the north) left each year in search of work.[9] Even in the 1950s over half of the male heads of household were absent from Peñasco from six to nine months of the year.[10]

In the 1940s Peñasco, Chamisal and other similar communities boasted a disproportionately small number of resident men between the ages of twenty-five and fifty-four.[11] More and more the population came to be made up of the very young and the very old, making further inroads into local agricultural and pastoral production. Those who remained grew increasingly dependent on the outside sources of income. Work within the area was chronically scarce, and the percentage of people in all of Taos County who were employed between 1950 and 1960 was more than twenty-six percent lower than the state level.[12] The result has been a very low standard of living for most residents and a high degree of dependence on government work and relief.

In 1940, Lee documented Peñasco and Chamisal in the midst of this mounting crisis. The impact of land loss severely affected village life although "practically all of the people" still relied to some extent on agriculture and many retained small herds of livestock.[13] During the Depression, area income from migratory labor had been reduced by as much as eighty percent,[14] and most workers had returned home. Poverty was acute, starvation prevented only by government job programs, food distribution and relief payments.[15] Still, family members had returned from afar, commercial pressures had waned temporarily, and everyone concentrated on producing everything possible from the land.

When I visited Peñasco and Chamisal during the summer of 1981, residents invited me into their homes with the same hospitality they must have shown Lee. Then as now, they are interested in articulating the nature of their communities' past and present. I showed photocopies of thirty-five Lee photographs to a range of individuals over fifty years of age, noting identifications of persons, places and activities, and I tape-recorded extensive accounts of life around 1940.

Three themes emerge most clearly from these interviews: *cooperation, respect for the land,* and *independence.* Lee was able to grasp these values and to convey them visually, for example, in the photograph of the Domínguez family loading a horse-drawn mower into their treasured 1937 Ford pickup (Plate 18). Candido, Salomón and Benjamín (from left to right) labor under the watchful eye of their grandfather, José Frésquez.

The people helped each other. If someone was going to weed his fields, the people went to help him. There were no wages, nobody worked for wages. They just went and helped each other. Not any more. Now if you want someone to help you, they say "how much do you pay?"[16]

Family members, even if married and living in separate households, would join together in plowing, planting, weeding, and mowing or harvesting each field in turn.[17]

Cooperation was equally evident in the construction and repair of houses. Adobe bricks are made by pouring a mixture of mud and straw into molds. After they are thoroughly sun-dried, they are laid in rows on a mud-and-stone or, more recently, cement foundation and the whole covered with mud plaster. The roof is composed of heavy beams, rows of sticks, and several inches of mud. These stages in the construction of a house or church are commonly undertaken by men, while women take charge of applying several layers of mud plaster to the walls (Plates 32–38).

Both the raising and plastering (and periodic replastering) of walls necessitated the cooperation of many neighbors and/or relatives. As an elderly woman from Chamisal recalled:

They used to help me when I was plastering here; we never had to do it alone. They would help me for their part, and when one of them was going to plaster, the rest would help her, you see. They just helped, they weren't paid. But not now. Now you have to pay people.

Such occasions were not simply social in nature; they afforded opportunity for displaying technical virtuosity and a keen aesthetic sense. Cleofas López, for example, shown at work in Plate 37, was known as the best plasterer in Chamisal. Building adobe fireplaces, niches, shelves and so forth inside buildings (Plates 40, 41) also required great skill. These photographs enable us to see why such abilities were (and are) so greatly esteemed.

The church provided another center for cooperative activities. Many religious ceremonies were performed mainly or entirely by members of lay religious societies such as the Confraternity of Our Father Jesus and the Carmelites (Plates 80, 81). The feast day of the chapel's patron was an important one in the community. The Catholic chapel in Chamisal (Plate 83) is dedicated to the Holy Cross (La Santa Cruz). The Feast of the Holy Cross on May 3 was inaugurated with a mass and a bonfire-illuminated procession the previous night. A community-wide feast and dance, graced by fiddle and guitar, highlighted the feast day. Lay religious societies also assumed responsibility for baptisms, weddings, wakes and burials, bringing together neighbors and relatives to lend moral and material support in times of unusual joy or sorrow.

A second theme which emerges from the photographs and interviews is a great respect for the land. Rural Mexicanos from northern New Mexico have long cherished the life of the *ranchero*, the independent small-scale farmer and rancher. To provide for one's family's needs by tilling the soil and raising livestock earned a man his neighbor's esteem. The goal was not to be deemed *macho,* a term commonly used in the area only to refer to a mule, but to exhibit *hombría,* the independence achieved in providing for household necessities through hard work. Women aspired to being *mujerota,* fulfilling the female ideal by bearing and raising children, managing the household, helping with the farmwork and preparing the products of flocks and fields for consumption.

Elders today recall the pre-World War II period as a positive time, in large part because people were still closely bound to their land.

Life was a bit different than it is now. We got by with horses. The majority of the people had horses, and we worked the earth with horses and oxen. So we lived in the old way *(el estilo antiguo),* the hard way. We had kerosene lamps to light things up. The National Forest was there, but they still gave us some permits for fuelwood and everything, but not any more. We had goats, sheep, cattle; not too many cattle, more goats. And we had lots of horses. Everyone had flour. We didn't buy anything but matches, salt, baking soda, kerosene and coffee in the store. And we got by very well. We planted a lot of wheat, a lot of beans, corn, everything. Everything we needed to eat. We made *posole* (similar to hominy) and *chicos* (dried kernels of corn which are boiled). We ate *atole* (a thin gruel made from blue corn), horsebeans, boiled goatsmilk, garbanzos, goatmeat, beef, pork. We had storerooms *(dispensas)* which we filled with meat for the winter. And we dried meat, we dried everything.

We used to do our threshing with horses and with goats. We harvested the wheat with a sickle. Afterwards we cleaned off a fairly large area, then we added straw and water, so the ground would harden up. Once we saw that the dirt was not loose, we made piles of wheat, beans or horsebeans and we threshed them. We washed the wheat, and then we spread it out on cloths in the sun to dry. We had to wash it because, you see, a few rocks always got in while we were threshing it. We put the dry wheat in a sack and then we took it to the grist mill to grind it.

Horses were also used in pulling the hay mower and in transporting hay and alfalfa (Plate 13). The Mediterranean scratch plow, a shallow-cutting plow without a moldboard, was drawn by horses or oxen (Plate 17).

The narrator's stress on beasts of burden for agriculture and transportation is well placed. In succeeding decades the need for trucks, cars, and tractors increased the residents' need for cash income. Ironically, such efforts to foster agricultural productivity also forced people to derive more income from outside sources. The vehicles also decreased the "distance" between Chamisal, Peñasco, and the world beyond, facilitating migratory wage labor and even emigration. The loss of intimacy with the land is still keenly felt by those who remember:

Now the people hardly plant anything. We used to plant lots of corn, lots of wheat, lots. But now the fields don't produce like they used to. Why? Because God became angry with us. We are going in a very bad direction. We just want the easy way. The thing is also that the elders of bygone days used to plant a lot, but they helped each other, they had assistance. But now if people are going to plant, they say, "Why should I plant so much? I can't weed all that alone." So now a person doesn't plant too much, because there is no one to help you with the weeding. You don't raise enough to be able to pay people to help you, see what I mean? And I believe that that kind of help is worth more than anything, even money. Now money is hardly worth anything. And if we don't work the land, there won't be anything to buy. The Bible says that people will throw money away in the streets, because they won't find anything to buy with it. Yes, we are coming to the end of all this.

This "end" we are all approaching is at one level millennialist: the present age of corruption will be replaced by a time of perfection and the presence of the divine. However, the elderly Chamisal resident is also alluding to the displacement of two central elements in traditional Mexicano society—cooperation and attachment to the land.

Peñasco, Chamisal, and similar communities used to be very tightly woven. People saw one another on an almost daily basis. Trust in God's will and a willingness to help one's neighbors were prime values. Residents all held the belief that a living could be wrested from such a precarious environment only if all were committed to sharing their labor and goods. Once the periodic exodus of most men from the community became a necessity, however, such day-to-day cooperation was no longer possible.

Increasing involvement in modern society fostered individualism, a stress on the rights and obligations of the isolated person rather than the community. Absenteeism and a growing alienation from the land lessened the people's devotion to feasts, processions and wakes that celebrated God's and the saints' protection of flocks and fields and that symbolized community solidarity. Community-wide cooperation became less pervasive and working the land grew to be more a means to supplement wages and relief and to maintain a symbolic link to the life of the *ranchero*.

The ideal of living off the land was closely related to that of independence. Each household mustered labor and resources to provide for itself and the community. A major goal was to be able to *trabajar por sí mismo*, "to work for oneself." In this way one's security was ideally dependent only upon God's will and neither upon the availability of wage labor nor the whims of bosses, landlords, government administrators and others. One did not wish to be autonomous or isolated, a disastrous state of affairs, but to maintain one's sense of pride and self-sufficiency.

Lee's photographs capture this spirit of strong independence in various ways. The portraits, especially of elders such as José Frésquez (Plate 24) and Josefita Lovato (Plate 39), both of Chamisal, display the effects of toil and determination to secure a living from a semiarid land for over half a century. Juan Policarpio Abeyta, also of Chamisal, proudly wears his overalls and farmer's hat, attributes of the *ranchero* (Plate 66).

The independence which characterized the residents of Chamisal and Peñasco in 1940 and before is most clearly reflected in Lee's images of crafts and crafts production. In the nineteenth and earlier centuries, Mexicanos of northern New Mexico produced a wealth of carved, woven and otherwise handcrafted goods.[18] After the arrival of the railroads in the 1880s folk artists found they could not compete with the influx of mass-produced, "fashionable" goods. The need to devote increasing amounts of time to wage labor decreased the time which could be used to produce items already relatively inexpensive at the local general-merchandise store. Yet the satisfaction of creating works of art with one's own hands and the desire to remain as independent as possible from labor contractors and merchants remained strong. Lee's photographs of Gomisinda Martínez, affectionately known as "La Martina," washing wool by an irrigation ditch provide a most penetrating and aesthetic example of this persistence (Plate 45).

During the 1920s, 1930s, and the post-war period, old skills were also adapted to the new need to generate cash income. High schools, Depression-era vocational programs, and later veterans' programs gave residents opportunities to advance their handicraft skills and to receive training in the use of mechanized equipment. Tourism in the rural communities and especially in centers like Taos, Santa Fe and Albuquerque provided new market outlets.[19]

In Peñasco and Chamisal these trends can be seen most clearly in a resurgence of furniture production. One of the many community vocational schools administered by the State Supervisor of Trade and Industrial Education was located in Peñasco.[20] High school students also received training in woodworking techniques in the Menaul School, a mission school operated by the Presbyterian Church in Albuquerque. World War II veterans also received training in a government-sponsored program in Peñasco. Residents note that quite a number of men from both Chamisal and Peñasco produced furniture just before and just after the war.

Benjamín Domínguez, who is pictured in Plates 9 and 19, fashioned such items as book cases, beds, dressers, free-standing clothes closets, carved boxes, chairs and couches. He received his instruction both at Menaul and later in the veteran training program at Peñasco. He also learned from his grandfather, José Frésquez, himself an accomplished furniture maker. Lee photographed Frésquez holding an old hand plane (Plate 42). Grandson Benjamin also operated a small forge in his father's house. His blacksmithing efforts were devoted primarily to repairing farm tools, another example of applying traditional technologies to modern tasks. Domínguez has also produced furniture at home in subsequent years, and he still maintains a small shop.

Such furniture was intended for two audiences. Much of the work remained in the home of the artist or his family, with many pieces given to relatives. Domínguez recalls:

I never sold anything. The things that I made, I made for myself. I had all of my work here at home. When I was bringing my dresser from school in Menaul in our old pickup, they stopped us and offered me $300 cash for it. But I didn't want to sell it.

He still proudly displays the box shown in Plate 43.

Other craftsmen produced items for sale to tourists. They would either place them by the side of the road when visitors were likely to be passing or sell them from the local high school. The smaller carved boxes and knickknacks like those illustrated in Plate 44 appear to have been most readily saleable. Their work exhibits a combination of modern materials (milled lumber), techniques and equipment, with Mexicano designs and carving techniques.

Both the Lee photographs and my own interviews show a people committed to their vision of the right way to live and determined to maintain as many of their traditional values as possible, despite external pressures. The residents' ability to articulate their past and to compare it to the present shows that they think about these issues frequently, discuss them regularly, and have considerable interest in learning about them. They had never seen the photographs and did not even recall Lee's having taken them, but after forty-one years the elders could identify nearly all of Lee's subjects and the images elicited hours of detailed descriptions of the persons, places and events captured by Lee. The vividness with which they remember the past is even more impressive in view of the fact that external pressures have interfered with the residents' ability to live this life and express these values throughout much of this century.

It is clear that their past way of life has an important significance for our future. The residents of Chamisal, Peñasco, and similar communities have been questioning for more than a century trends toward materialism and alienation from land and community which have so dramatically altered the world today. The Mexicanos' values of cooperation, respect for the land, and freedom from external domination will hardly appeal to everyone, and we are no longer in a position to return en masse to a small-scale, subsistence-oriented way of life. However, a deeper understanding of how people lived in rural northern New Mexico can help us see more clearly who we are and where we are going. Russell Lee's photographs of Chamisal and Peñasco thus possess, beyond their historic and artistic value, a vital relevance for our contemporary situation.

NOTES

1. For brief summaries of the history of settlement in the area, see William deBuys, "Fractions of Justice: A Legal and Social History of the Las Trampas Land Grant, New Mexico," *New Mexico Historical Review* 56 (1981):71–97; and Manuel Antonio Ferrán, "Planning for Economic Development of Rural Northern New Mexico, with Emphasis on the Peñasco Valley, Taos County," Ph.D. dissertation, University of Oklahoma, 1969, pp. 71–80.

2. See Marc Simmons, "Settlement Patterns and Village Plans in Colonial New Mexico," *Journal of the West* 8 (1969):8. Good recent reviews of the historical, legal and social questions relating to the common lands are provided by Malcolm Ebright, "The San Joaquin Grant: Who Owned the Common Lands? A Historical-Legal Puzzle," *New Mexico Historical Review* 57 (1982):5–26; and John R. Van Ness, "Hispanic Village Organization in Northern New Mexico: Corporate Community Structure in Historical and Comparative Perspective," in Paul Kutsche, ed., *The Survival of Spanish American Villages,* The Colorado College Studies, no. 15, Colorado Springs, 1979, pp. 21–44.

3. See Article VIII of the treaty as reprinted in Richard N. Ellis, ed., *New Mexico Historical Documents* (Albuquerque: University of New Mexico Press, 1975), p. 14.

4. See John R. Van Ness, "Spanish American vs. Anglo American Land Tenure and the Study of Economic Change in New Mexico," *The Social Science Journal* 13 (1976):45–52. In "Las Trampas Land Grant," deBuys documents the manipulation of legal ambiguities by speculators in gaining control of a good share of the southern portion of the contiguous area.

5. See Interagency Council for Area Development Planning and the New Mexico State Planning Office, *Embudo: A Pilot Planning Project for the Embudo Watershed of New Mexico* (Santa Fe, 1962), Map 7, p. 21.

6. Ferrán, "Planning for Economic Development," p. 80.

7. Marc Simmons, *Spanish Government in New Mexico* (Albuquerque: University of New Mexico Press, 1968), pp. 90–100.

8. Interagency Council, *Embudo,* p. 8.

9. Allan G. Harper, Andrew R. Córdova and Kalvero Oberg, *Man and Resources in the Middle Rio Grande Valley* (Albuquerque: University of New Mexico Press, 1943), p. 63.

10. Bernard J. Siegel, "Some Structure Implications for Change in Pueblo and Spanish New Mexico," in Verne F. Ray, ed., *Intermediate Societies, Social Mobility, and Communication* (Seattle: American Ethnological Society, 1959), p. 39.

11. Ferrán, "Planning for Economic Development," p. 80; Interagency Council, *Embudo*, p. 26.

12. Ibid., *Embudo*, p. 32.

13. Marta Weigle, ed., *Hispanic Villages of Northern New Mexico* (Santa Fe, New Mexico: Lightning Tree, 1975), p. 208.

14. Soil Conservation Service, U.S. Department of Agriculture, *Village Livelihood in the Upper Rio Grande Area and a Note on the Level of Village Livelihood in the Upper Rio Grande Area* (Regional Bulletin No. 44, Conservation Economics Series No. 171, Soil Conservation Service, Albuquerque, 1937), p. 5.

15. Weigle, *Hispanic Villages*, p. 210.

16. This and the following quotations are my translations of excerpts from the Spanish transcriptions.

17. Students of Mexicano society have often commented on the deleterious effect of the Hispanic tradition of partible inheritance, dividing estates equally among the children (e.g., Interagency Council, *Embudo*, p. 19). While it is true that this can result in the fragmentation of fields' *ownership*, it had less effect on their utilization. Fences were few and family members' plots were generally worked as a unit. (I am indebted on this point to John R. Van Ness.)

18. See E. Boyd, *Popular Arts of Spanish New Mexico* (Santa Fe, New Mexico: Museum of New Mexico Press, 1974) for a discussion of Mexicano architecture, image-making, weaving and other arts.

19. On the production of handicrafts in the twentieth century for outside-oriented markets see Charles L. Briggs, *The Wood Carvers of Córdova, New Mexico: Social Dimensions of an Artistic "Revival"* (Knoxville: University of Tennessee Press, 1980); Sarah Nestor, *The Native Market of the Spanish New Mexican Craftsmen, Santa Fe, 1933–1940* (Santa Fe, New Mexico: Colonial New Mexico Historical Foundation, 1978); Marta Weigle, "The First Twenty-Five Years of the Spanish Colonial Arts Society" in idem with Claudia Larcombe and Samuel Larcombe, eds., *Hispanic Arts and Ethnohistory in the Southwest: New Papers Inspired by the Work of E. Boyd* (Santa Fe: Ancient City Press; Albuquerque: University of New Mexico Press, 1983) pp. 181–203; and the articles in William Wroth, ed., *Hispanic Crafts of the Southwest* (Colorado Springs, Colorado: The Taylor Museum of the Colorado Springs Fine Arts Center, 1977).

20. See, e.g., Mary W. Coan, "Handicraft Arts Revived," *New Mexico Magazine*, February 1934, p. 14; Wayne Mauzy, "Santa Fe's Native Market," *El Palacio* 40 (1936):64–72; William Wroth, "New Hope in Hard Times: Hispanic Crafts Are Revived During Troubled Years," *El Palacio* 89, 2 (Summer 1983):22–31.

Taos

Chamisal • • Peñasco

Santa Fe

Albuquerque

Grande

Rio

NEW MEXICO

THE PLATES

The 86 photographs in this section have been selected from the more than 250 taken by Russell Lee during his visit to Chamisal and Peñasco in July 1940. They were chosen to provide an overview of the way of life and daily activities of village residents at that time. The pictures are divided into seven groups: The Villages, Farming, Adobe Construction, Handicrafts, Domestic Scenes and Activities, The Outside World, and Religion. Lee's excellent portraits of the villagers are interspersed. Both the selection and the grouping are intended to reflect the systematic and comprehensive coverage of all aspects of village life that Lee made during his brief visit.

Since Lee seldom took an uninteresting or poorly composed photograph, the process of selection for this book was a difficult one; many of the photographs still in the files are equal in aesthetic quality and importance to the ones reproduced here. The negatives for these and all the FSA photographs are preserved by the Prints and Photographs Division of the Library of Congress, where custom prints were made by the Photoduplication Service for reproduction in this volume. In 1942, the FSA Historical Section, which was responsible for the original prints and negatives, was transferred to the Domestic Branch of the United States Office of War Information, where the documentary work continued for two more years. In 1944, by Executive Order, all negatives from the FSA and OWI photographic projects were deposited in the Library of Congress, a welcome move that insured their preservation for future generations.

The following plates are accompanied by the Library of Congress negative numbers and the original captions which Jean Lee, Russell Lee's wife, made for each photograph. After 1938, Mrs. Lee travelled with her husband on their FSA and later photographic assignments and recorded accurate captions for virtually every one of Lee's many photographs.

In some cases that follow, Jean Lee's captions are amended by italicized editorial comments identifying subjects when possible and giving background on some of the activities and artifacts in the photographs. Many of these comments are in the present tense, for some aspects of life in Chamisal and Peñasco have changed but little since July 1940. Residents and former residents of Chamisal and Peñasco, who were interviewed by Charles L. Briggs and William Wroth, identified subjects in the photographs.

THE VILLAGES

1. Peñasco *vicinity*, Taos County, New Mexico. Rural scene. *LC-USF 34-37430.*

2. Chamisal. Main Street. *LC-USF 34-37009.*

3. Chamisal. Farmstead of a Spanish-American farmer. *Many of the homes in Chamisal are small* ranchos *situated in or close to farming lands. LC-USF 34-37100.*

4. Peñasco. Adobe house. *A more "urban" mode of architecture—the row house facing the main street—is found in Peñasco. LC-USF 34-37180.*

5. Chamisal. Home of Spanish-American farmers. *LC-USF 34-37126*.

6. Chamisal. Home of a Spanish-American farmer. *LC-USF 34-37134*.

7. Peñasco. Main Street. *LC-USF 34-37174.*

8. Peñasco. Filling station is the only building of modern design in this Spanish-American village. *While Chamisal is a farming community, Peñasco is somewhat larger and serves as the trading center for the area. LC-USF 34-37161.*

9. Peñasco. Blacksmith shop. *LC-USF 34-37177*.

10. Chamisal. Family group of Spanish-Americans. *Four generations. From left: José Frésquez, Cipriano Domínguez, Salomón Domínguez, Sr., Salomón Domínguez, Jr. LC-USF 33-12820-M2.*

FARMING

11. Chamisal. Garden and orchard of a Spanish-American farmer. Notice the revetment at the left to prevent the stream from cutting further into the bank. *The revetment was constructed by the U.S. Soil Conservation Service in the 1930s as part of their agricultural rehabilitation program. LC-USF 33-37133.*

12. Chamisal. Spanish-American farmer pitching hay. *Hand methods are still often used today. LC-USF 34-37105.*

13. Chamisal. Pitching hay on a Spanish-American farm. *LC-USF 34-37139.*

14. Chamisal. Driving cows. *LC-USF 33-12841-M5*.

15. Peñasco. Child tending cows which are grazing along irrigation ditch. *LC-USF 33-12804-M1*.

16. Peñasco. Young Spanish-American cow herder. *LC-USF 33-12804-M3*.

17. Chamisal. Spanish-American farmer with wooden plow which was used by his father. *LC-USF 34-37014.*

18. Chamisal. Spanish-American farmers loading a mower onto a truck. *The Domínguez family. From left, the brothers Candido, Salomón and Benjamín, supervised by their grandfather, José Frésquez. LC-USF 33-12802-M1.*

19. Chamisal. Corn and beans grown by the Spanish-Americans. *Corn and beans were traditional staple crops of the region and are still grown on a small scale today.* LC-USF 33-12806-M2.

20. Chamisal. Spanish-American boy weeding the garden. *LC-USF 34-12813-M4*.

21. Chamisal. Spanish-American farmer. *Luis Lucero, a* ranchero *from the tiny neighboring community of Ojitos. LC-USF 33-12822-M4.*

22. Chamisal. Adobe shed and barn of a Spanish-American. *LC-USF 34-37055*.

23. Chamisal. Logs are transported in the Spanish-American country by means of horse and chain. *Trucks now are almost universally used. LC-USF 33-12839-M2.*

24. Chamisal. Spanish-American farmer. *José Frésquez. LC-USF 33-12820-M1.*

25. Chamisal. Spanish-American farmer whetting his knife.
LC-USF 33012839-M5.

26. Chamisal. Spanish-American farmer slaughtering a hog. *LC-USF 33-12839-M4.*

27. Chamisal. Removing the liver from a slaughtered hog. *LC-USF 33-12846-M2.*

28. Chamisal. Spanish-American farmer washing his hands after dressing a hog. *LC-USF 33-12843-M1.*

29. Chamisal. Spanish-American farmer with the head of a slaughtered hog. *LC-USF 33-12843-M3.*

30. Chamisal. Spanish-American woman hanging up meat to dry. *LC-USF 33-12833-M2.*

31. Chamisal. Spanish-American
boy. *LC-USF 34-12822-M3.*

32. Chamisal. Spanish-American removing form-shaped adobe brick. The adobe brick is dried next by the sun. *LC-USF 33-12819-M3.*

33. Peñasco. Removing the rough edges from an adobe brick with a trowel. *LC-USF 33-12826-M4.*

34. Peñasco. Using a level in constructing a window opening of an adobe house. *The adobe mason is Jim Martínez, of Peñasco, now said to be living in Denver. LC-USF 33-12825-M3.*

35. Chamisal. Mixing straw with mud to make the plaster which is used to re-plaster the houses each year. *LC-USF 34-37051*.

36. Chamisal. Spanish-American woman plastering an adobe house. *LC-USF 33-12823-M1*.

37. Chamisal. After the plaster is applied with a trowel, it is smoothed out with the hands. The women pride themselves on careful plastering. *Cleofas López. Considered to have been the best plasterer in Chamisal. In this photograph the adobe is being applied by hand, to be smoothed later with the trowel. LC-USF 34-12811-M5.*

38. Chamisal. Spanish-American women replastering an adobe house. This is done once a year. *LC-USF 34-37082*.

39. Chamisal. Spanish-American women. *Josafita Lovato. LC-USF 33-12836-M1.*

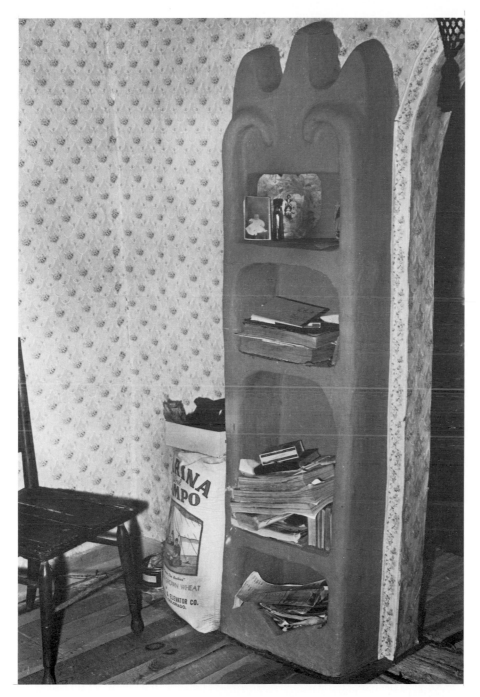

40. Chamisal. Adobe cupboard of a Spanish-American farm. *The adobe shelves in this and the next plate are especially elaborate and finely crafted. They are excellent examples of the little-known art of Hispanic women plasterers (enjarradoras).* *LC-USF 34-37027.*

41. Chamisal. Wife of a Spanish-American family arranging things in an adobe cupboard which she designed and built. *Evangelina López of Chamisal. This mantle or shelf* (repisa) *appears to have been inspired by the traditional* fogón, *cooking fireplace used prior to the introduction of the cast iron stove. An identical* repisa *graced the other side of the doorway in this home. LC-USF 34-37017.*

HANDICRAFTS

42. Chamisal. Old Spanish-American farmer with his homemade tools. *José Frésquez was an accomplished carpenter and furniture-maker. LC-USF 34-37025.*

43. Chamisal. Spanish-American boy with a chest which he carved. These people are adept in many of the handicrafts. *Benjamín Domínguez. LC-USF 34-36986.*

44. Chamisal. Spanish-American men with examples of their wood carving which they hope to sell to tourists. *From left: Eugenio Arrellano, possibly Rumaldo Córdova, and Ernestino Arrellano. LC-USF 34-37603.*

45. Chamisal. Old Spanish-American woman. *Gomasínda Martínez, washing wool in the irrigation ditch LC-USF 33-12817-M5.*

46. Chamisal. Spanish-American girl washing wool. *LC-USF 33-12817-M4.*

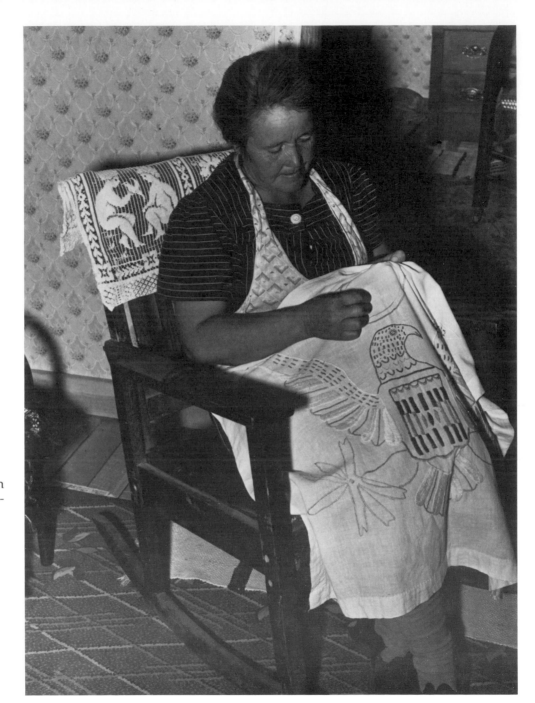

47. Chamisal. Spanish-American woman doing needlework. *Evangelina López. LC-USF 34-37017.*

48. Chamisal. Spanish-American
farmer repairing his wife's shoes.
Diego Lovato. LC-USF 34-37018.

49. Chamisal. Spanish-American girls. *LC-USF 33-12835-M4*.

DOMESTIC SCENES
AND ACTIVITIES

50. Chamisal. Entrance to a Spanish-American house. *LC-USF 34-37102.*

51. Chamisal. Spanish-American farmer and his family. *LC-USF 34-37023.*

52. Chamisal. Spanish-American family eating dinner. *LC-USF 34-37006*.

53. Chamisal. Corner of a room in the home of a Spanish-American farmer. *Two important images of the Blessed Virgin grace the walls of this room: Our Lady of Mt. Carmel on the left and Our Lady of Guadalupe on the right. The doorway to the closet on the right is a delicately modeled and outlined arch of adobe. Probably the home of Ontoniel and Evangelina López. LC-USF 34-37019.*

54. Chamisal. Spanish-American farmer and his family. *Ontoniel and Evangelina López with children. LC-USF 34-37146.*

55. Chamisal. Spanish-American farmer and his daughter seated on the couch which his son built at the school workshop in Albuquerque. *Ontoniel López. Note also handmade table, small chest and standing ashtray, and the handwoven couch covers. LC-USF 34-37170.*

56. Chamisal. Detail of a bedroom of a Spanish-American farmer with homemade tools (sic). *Perhaps "toys" is meant. LC-USF 34-37020.*

57. Chamisal. Spanish-American couple preparing fruit for canning. *LC-USF 34-37098.*

58. Chamisal. Spanish-American boy eating sweet corn which he has roasted on top of a hot stove. *Note the pressure cooker for canning on the stove. LC-USF 34-37130.*

59. Chamisal. Removing jars of canned fruit from a pressure cooker. *LC-USF 34-37036.*

60. Chamisal. Outside adobe oven of Spanish-American family. *The* horno, *used for baking bread and roasting corn, is of Moorish origin and came to New Mexico with the Spanish Conquest. It is still commonly used by both the Hispanic villagers and the Pueblo Indians. LC-USF 34-36985.*

61. Chamisal. Spanish-American boy playing horse. *LC-USF 34-12809-M3*.

62. Chamisal. Spanish-American boy drawing water from a well. *LC-USF 34-37000.*

63. Chamisal. Daughter of a Spanish-American farmer washing. *LC-USF 33-12820-M4.*

64. Chamisal. Spanish-American boy dipping water from an irrigating ditch. Water will be used in the house for cooking, drinking, etc. *LC-USF 33-12821-M3*.

65. Chamisal. Spanish-American boy playing in an irrigation ditch. *LC-USF 34-12816-M3*.

66. Chamisal. Major-domo, who has charge of irrigation water rights and problems. *Juan Policarpío Abeyta, Chamisal* ranchero, *was a highly regarded member of the community.* LC-USF 34-12822-M3.

67. Chamisal. Spanish-American boy. *LC-USF 33-12836-M4.*

THE OUTSIDE WORLD

68. Chamisal. Spanish-American farmer standing in front of an adobe wall. *LC-USF 33-12815-M5.*

69. Peñasco. The mail comes into town in this light wagon. *LC-USF 33-12837-M4*.

70. Chamisal. Spanish-American women waiting to see the doctor at the travelling clinic which comes from the Presbyterian Hospital at Embudo. *From left: Evangelina López, Felicita Frésquez de Domínguez (daughter of José Frésquez), Julia Rodriguez, Elvira Córdova, Lucia Archuleta. All are residents of Chamisal. LC-USF 34-37168.*

71. Chamisal. Spanish-American women waiting to see the doctor at the travelling clinic which comes from the Presbyterian Hospital at Embudo. *LC-USF 34-37144*.

72. Chamisal. Spanish-American woman being examined in the travelling clinic which comes from the Presbyterian Hospital in Embudo. *Felicita Frésquez de Domínguez. LC-USF 34-37143.*

73. Chamisal. Spanish-American farmer who is also justice of the peace and teacher in the local grade school. *LC-USF 34-12825-M4.*

74. Peñasco. Barkeeper. *LC-USF 34-37211.*

75. Peñasco. Poster of travelling Spanish-American show. *Travelling shows were a traditional form of entertainment for the isolated villages, dating back to the colonial period. They were usually variety shows such as this one, and originally often included puppets (los titeres) and other distractions for children. LC-USF 33-12821-M1.*

76. Peñasco. Orchestra playing in front of the hall to attract a crowd to the show. *LC-USF 34-37097.*

77. Peñasco. Audience of Spanish-Americans at a travelling show. *The two men in the center are Miguel González on the left and Epifanio Chacón on the right.* LC-USF 34-37095.

78. Peñasco. Spanish-American clowns at a travelling show. *LC-USF 34-37099.*

79. Peñasco. Spanish-American acrobat of the travelling show and the audience in the background. LC-USF 34-37094.

RELIGION

80. Peñasco. Procession of Spanish-American Catholics to honor a saint. *The women in the front carry a banner displaying the image of Our Lady of Carmel, which suggests that it is her feast day, July 16, and that these women are* carmelitas, *members of the lay order dedicated to this advocation of Our Lady. The second banner displays Our Lady of Guadalupe and the third is another image of the Blessed Virgin. The church of San Antonio in the background burned in 1961 and was replaced by the present one. LC-USF 34-37147.*

81. Peñasco. Spanish-American man leading the Catholic procession held in honor of a saint. *The leader carrying the processional cross is Facundo Medina of Peñasco. The elderly woman immediately to his left is Margarita Martínez. In the background is the general merchandise store owned by Ramón Sánchez (d. 1923), which went out of business in the mid-1930s. LC-USF 33-12827-M2.*

82. Peñasco. Bringing up the rear of a Spanish-American Catholic procession held to honor a saint. *LC-USF 33-12828-M5*.

83. Chamisal. Catholic Church. *It was built in the mid-1930s to replace the original nineteenth-century church which was in poor condition.* *LC-USF 34-36993.*

84. Chamisal. Spanish-Americans. *On the left is Rebecca Martínez de López. LC-USF 33-12828-M1.*

85. Peñasco. Monument in a Catholic cemetery. The monument was donated by a local rich man. *Grave of Ramón Sánchez. LC-USF 34-37156.*

86. Peñasco. Entrance to the cemetery. *LC-USF 34-37160.*

"TAKING PICTURES OF THE HISTORY OF TODAY": RUSSELL LEE'S PHOTOGRAPHY

Alan M. Fern and William Wroth

. . . Whenever they asked me "What are you doing out here taking pictures?" I said, "Well, I'm taking pictures of the history of today." And they understood this. And this was an entree to the people that were difficult to communicate with. . . . I sort of felt, too, that by means of these pictures we were helping some . . . parts of the country understand what the other parts . . . were like. People just hadn't traveled over this country in those days the way they have now. The roads were not as good.
—From an interview with Russell Lee, June 2, 1964.

Russell Lee first came to public notice in the late 1930s as one of the small group of photographers hired by the federal government's new Farm Security Administration to document conditions in the United States, particularly in rural areas devastated by drought, flood, and poor farming practices. The historical unit of the FSA was headed by Roy Stryker, who hired Lee in 1936, following a recommendation from his friend, the painter Ben Shahn, who had already done photographic work for Stryker. Stryker himself had come to Washington from Columbia University at the invitation of Rexford Guy Tugwell, one of President Franklin D. Roosevelt's New Deal "brain trusters." Both Stryker and Tugwell hoped to supply pictures to new publications like *Life*, thereby giving a national forum for the Roosevelt administration. They also hoped to create exhibitions from the photographs they assembled and to show them in areas as yet unaware of the gravity of the agricultural problem in the nation.

At Columbia University in the early 1920s, Roy Stryker and his mentor, Rexford Guy Tugwell, had started to collect pictorial documentation to support their teaching and study of economics. In this, they were following in the tradition of socially concerned documentary photography begun in New York City by late nineteenth- and early twentieth-century pioneers like Jacob Riis and Lewis Hine. During the 1920s, journals like *Survey Graphic*, which made use of photographic essays on social issues, and groups like the Photo League of New York, which encouraged photographers to address themselves to socially meaningful work, were exploring the potential of the photograph as a tool for communication.

Stryker later recalled that "in 1936 photography, which theretofore had been mostly a matter of landscapes and snapshots and family portraits, was fast being discovered as a serious tool of communication, a new way for a thoughtful, creative person to make a statement."[1] His dismissal of the pictorial use of photography reflects an attitude that had developed within a few decades after the invention of the photographic process in the 1830s. Those who attempted the new craft had soon become aware of its artistic potential. Although it appeared that the camera could serve as a perfectly neutral recording medium, the truth was that the photographer had to select the scene to be recorded, choose the focal length of the lens (thus affecting the importance given to objects before the camera), and consider the appearance of the finished photograph by the exposure and development given to the photosensitive material. Thus, photographers with some sophistication in other visual arts realized the possibilities in the creative range afforded by the medium, and some even regarded their work in the same way painters did.

Toward the end of the nineteenth century, following the course set by such photographers as Henry P. Robinson, P. H. Emerson, and O. J. Rejlander in England and Alfred Stieglitz and his colleagues in the United States, a clearly defined movement in artistic photography emerged. Journals were devoted to the publication of expressive work, and exhibitions brought the prints of these photographers before the public. "Creative" photographers such as Paul Strand, Gertrude Kasebier, Clarence White, and many others took their work in directions similar to painters of their time who were exploring the effects of light on form and texture and seeking formal equivalents for states of emotion. By the 1930s, Ansel Adams, Edward Weston, and other photographers in America and Europe whose work is well known today had joined the ranks of those who regarded their work as "creative" and made their statements in aesthetic terms.

By the mid-1930s, however, Henry Luce was planning a new magazine—to be known as *Life*—that would be devoted entirely to the picture story, using it as magazines previously had used the written word—to inform and persuade a mass audience about issues of significance in the world. *Life* thus followed another direction in photography, one which started in 1855 with the Crimean War coverage by Roger Fenton, the Civil War reportage by Mathew B. Brady and his associates, and the photographers who accompanied explorers in the American West and the Middle East. Through publications illustrated with original prints of their work, and through books like Smith and Thompson's *Street Life in London* (1877) and Thomas Annan's 1868 studies for the City of Glasgow Improvement Trust, the power of the photograph as a recording medium was made manifest. It was in this tradition that the Danish-American journalist Jacob Riis and his younger contemporary Lewis Hine began their work, the former in the 1880s, the latter in the early 1900s. Even though Riis's photographs were published as rather dim reproductions accompanying his articles on tenement life in New York City, such was the power of his observation that he was credited with bringing about significant changes in housing laws and health regulations and winning sympathy for the plight of young workers. His photographs for the National Child Labor Committee helped bring about reforms in the employment of children.

Agricultural problems were the specialty of Rexford Tugwell from his days teaching economics at Columbia University. His theories on rural poverty stimulated Roosevelt, who brought him to Washington in 1933 as an advisor and as assistant secretary of agriculture. A number of Columbia people followed, including Tugwell's former assistant, Roy Stryker. In the summer of 1934, Stryker took a temporary job in the Information Division of the Agricultural Adjustment Administration, where he had access to the picture file of the Department of Agriculture. Late that summer, he approached Tugwell: " 'You know, Rex, all those pictures are just sitting down there going to waste. Why don't we do a picture book on agriculture?' Tugwell quickly saw the direction of Stryker's mind and grasped the possibilities. 'It's a good idea,' he said, 'and you could go even further and make it a picture *source* book on agriculture.' "[2] Stryker began outlining the book and continued work on it after returning to teach at Columbia.

The Resettlement Administration was established when Executive Order 7027 was signed by President Roosevelt on April 30, 1935. Tugwell was to be chief of the new agency, which was to handle low-interest loans to poor farmers, soil rebuilding, reforestation and other conservation projects, and various resettlement projects in experimental communal farms and more conventional rural communities. Tugwell created an Information Division to publicize the program's accomplishment and asked Stryker to serve as chief of the division's historical section to "direct the activities of investigators, photographers, economists, sociologists and statisticians engaged in the accumulation and compilation of reports . . ., statistics, photographic material, vital statistics, agricultural surveys, maps and sketches necessary to make accurate descriptions of the various . . . phases of the Resettlement Administration, particularly with regard to the historical, sociological and economic aspects of the several programs and their accomplishments."[3] It soon became apparent to Stryker that the agency's photographic work was haphazard and counterproductive, and he approached Tugwell, who issued an order giving Stryker full responsibility for all Resettlement Administration photodocumentary work.

In 1937, the Resettlement Administration was absorbed into the U.S. Department of Agriculture and renamed the Farm Security Administration. Tugwell resigned, but Stryker continued to direct the historical section, which by then included several photographers. Stryker had managed to hire photographers and assign them to field work recording the aggravated condition of poor farmers and farm laborers as early as 1935. At that time, he recalled, "I had no idea what was going to happen. I did not expect to be shocked at what began to come across my desk. . . . Every day was for me an education and a revelation. I could hardly wait to get to the mail in the morning."[4] Throughout his years in Washington, Stryker maintained an ulterior purpose for the incoming photographs, holding "onto a personal dream that inevitably got translated into black-and-white pictures: I wanted to do a personal encyclopedia of American agriculture." Thus, in his instructions for the field photographers he included such footnotes as "Keep your eyes open for a rag doll and a corn tester," and such directions "undoubtedly accounted for the great number of photographs that got into the collection which had nothing to do with official business."[5]

Russell Lee was peculiarly fitted to work with Stryker's small but vigorous group of photographers. Born on July 21, 1903, at Ottawa, Illinois, he grew up in a town amid farming communities. Although he did not live on a farm, some of his relatives did, and by the time he went off to school he was familiar with the life and routines of the rural midwest. Trained as a chemical engineer at Lehigh University, he took a job in a small manufacturing company after graduation.

Lee married an art student, Doris Emrick, and soon found himself surrounded by painters. Increasingly attracted by the challenges of the visual arts, he left his job as plant manager in 1929 and went to study painting at the California School of Fine Arts. About this time, a small inheritance made it possible for him to follow his own inclinations and to leave the world of commerce.

From California the Lees moved to Woodstock, New York, a community on the Hudson River above New York City that had attracted a number of serious artists. One of their friends, Emil Ganso, had a 35mm camera, and Lee tried it out. Almost at once he realized that photography, not painting, was his medium.

Although Lee was largely self taught as a photographer, his understanding of chemistry and optics and his painter's command of composition provided him with a solid technical and aesthetic basis. He began to photograph country auctions and other local events. He also recorded the people of Manhattan, especially some of the followers of the Black preacher Father Divine just coming to prominence in Harlem.

When the Lees first moved to Woodstock the brash optimism of the 1920s was still the prevailing mood. Among artists, the most serious debates centered on the achievement of a genuinely American style and how to respond to the powerful and unconventional departures of the French and German painters who dominated the international art world. Doris Lee's work was allied more closely to that of Grant Wood and Thomas Hart Benton than to Picasso or Paul Klee, and Russell's work as a photographer began to reflect a similar preoccupation with the American scene.

By 1935, for Russell Lee and for many of his friends, it was no longer possible to think of art for art's sake. They realized photography in particular could play a significant part in the shaping of public opinion and in recording the conditions that responsible citizens ought to understand. In the summer of 1936, Lee recalled, "a visiting friend, Joe Jones, a painter originally from St. Louis, came up to Woodstock, and he told us of an exhibition of photographs by a government group. I was going to New York anyway, so I took a look at this, and I . . . said 'Well, I ought to meet these people.' So I went down to Washington."[6] There he met Stryker, who appreciated Lee's work and hired him after Carl Mydans left in the fall of 1936.

The work with Stryker delighted Lee. He reported that "Stryker just gave us our heads, and just a little direction after we'd sort of proven ourselves. . . . He'd always put suggestions in his letters. We'd get these letters which would be ten, twelve handwritten pages, something like that. We might get one a week, or every ten days . . . and his observations about the pictures that I had been taking, pictures that Arthur [Rothstein] might have been taking, what Marion Wolcott might have been taking . . . or what Walker Evans was commenting upon. . . . It was very valuable to note these . . . we gleaned from this new things and felt quite a part of this whole, of the group, even though we seldom got together."[7] Lee entered into this effort with great enthusiasm.

Hiring Lee was fortuitous for Stryker; from the beginning they got along extremely well. Lee took criticisms and suggestions gracefully, with great concern to perform the job according to Stryker's wishes. After Lee had been on the job for two months, working in Iowa and Illinois, Stryker gave him his first critique:

In general I have one criticism to make; namely that perhaps you have not told as full a story as you might have in some of your sets. Would it not be better to have taken fewer families and spent more time with each, getting a fuller collection of pictures in each case? You have done many pictures of the families standing in front of their house or shack. They appear a bit stiff taken in this manner. These would be all right, provided we could show members of the same family in the house and doing various things. . . . In the balance of your work in Illinois, I would recommend that you cover less ground, but do it more intensively.[8]

Lee's response to this initial critique was immediate and positive:

Your criticism of my work is excellent. It was my idea while there to obtain pictures for the files on all different classifications of ownership and tenancy in the representative areas. It would have been more effective had I concentrated as you suggested. I shall do this in my work in Illinois.[9]

Stryker's criticism here established a format which Lee was to follow with outstanding results through the next five years: detailed and thorough photographic documentation of rural and town families in their daily lives. Stryker also emphasized the need for the photographer to understand the broader significance of what he was seeing, not simply to photograph whatever came before the camera and expect to present a coherent and meaningful picture of a culture. Lee's important surveys of communities such as Chamisal and Peñasco, St. Augustine, Texas, and Pie Town, New Mexico, attest to his comprehension of what Stryker wanted and his ability to carry it out.

Stryker not only provided general guidance for his photographers and critiques of their work, but he also gave them detailed outlines of what to photograph, right down to specific types of people, situations, and objects, with instructions as to *how* these things should be represented. Writing Lee in April 1937, Stryker gave him a full set of suggestions which he was to follow in documenting a "cut-over" area in the forestry-based economy of northern Michigan:

As I see the thing here, may I suggest some of the things that come to my mind. First, you will want, of course to get some 5 × 7 shots showing the look of the country—stumps, brush, scraggly trees, and so on; houses—inside and out; barns, outbuildings, and fences. Make a few photographic notes on the type of construction. These should be close-ups. If it is log, you should show whether there is anything in the way the logs have been put up. The interiors should show the furniture (or lack of furniture), and interior finish, plaster, wallpapers, newspapers and so forth. Get pictures of people in and out of their homes. Try to get some good interiors of school houses with school in session, and some shots of churches. We should like pictures of stores. Try to show the types of things they have for sale on their shelves—groceries, patent medicines.[10]

Stryker not only specified the types of shots he wanted but also the style in which they should be taken. As his letters to the photographers clearly indicate, he was well aware of both the powerful message of the documentary photograph and the ability of the photographer to alter or enhance that message. Stryker's letters to Lee often included requests for certain types of images that would convey a particular message, and even included instructions for achieving these desired results. In June 1937 he suggested to Lee that in his documentation of the Forest Products Lab in Michigan he "ought to take a few additional pictures of the *Fortune-Life* type which presents accurately the operation in question and over-dramatizes the man and/or microscope by lights, by cock-eyed angles or any other devise. If you have time to look through some of the copies of *Fortune*, you will get what I mean, I am sure. . . ."[11] Stryker then went on in his letter to list the specific shots he wished Lee to get in this manner, and Lee obliged accordingly.

Later, when Lee was working in the Southwest, Stryker suggested he shoot a few "Westons," that is, photographs in Edward Weston's style, to appease certain program critics and doubters. Weston's elegant Southwestern landscape photography was then receiving quite a bit of critical acclaim.

When you get to Arizona and New Mexico . . . as I suggested once before, even try a few *"Westons" by Russell Lee*. You have no idea how important these highly pictorial syrupy pictures are going to be, especially when some one comes in here who isn't particularly sold on our other photography, and is in a position to go out and do a lot of talking. New Mexico, Arizona and Utah and the rest of the country do have some skies filled with white clouds, so you had better get that red filter out. However, you damn well better not go too far, and spoil the picture.[12]

Lee for the most part carried out Stryker's wishes with incredible precision; Stryker's letters to him are full of laudatory comments. As early as January 1937 he could write: "We all want to compliment you on the most excellent stuff that came through on the last Contax rolls . . . the sharpest and clearest I have seen on miniature film for some time," and ten months later he would write, "I am delighted with the last two groups of pictures. The $3\frac{1}{4} \times 4\frac{1}{4}$ pictures are sharp, clear, and the subject matter exciting as hell."[13]

Lee's letters, like those from other FSA photographers, were important too. In the 1930s Washington was still quite removed from the concerns of American rural life. Communication systems were inadequate, roads were often bad and travel difficult. Letters from field photographers brought fresh news of the provinces to the central agency. Lee complied with Stryker's insistence that he inform himself about the background of what he was shooting, and his letters constituted well-organized and highly detailed field reports on the areas he was visiting, giving not only factual data but also a sense of the temper and level of frustration of the people. This information was especially valuable in determining what programs were needed in a particular area. In one of his early letters to Stryker, Lee gave a full report on farm tenancy problems in Iowa, outlining "Types of Tenancy," "Types of Leases," "Types of Landlords," and other relevant information. He included a county map on which he had sketched drought areas and the farm population.

The plight of rural Americans was forcefully brought home to Stryker and his associates in Washington by comments like the following by Lee:

There are several destitute families since W.P.A. work has stopped. In the opinion of these local men there is danger of an uprising among the farmers here unless immediate aid is forthcoming. Many families are living on potatoes, bread and gravy.[14]

In September 1937, Lee gave a long report on conditions among Mexican beetworkers in Minnesota, followed by information about a rift in the Farm-Labor party in the area—"sabotaged by Trotzkyites," according to its leaders, followed by a report that the mayor of Minneapolis was attempting to take younger single men and women off relief and put them into work camps—"looks like Fascist enterprise." This letter concluded: "Will try to get more dope [on these events] for you. . . . Rioting or uprising, incidently, is expected in Western North Dakota."[15]

Lee not only provided field information, but with his background in chemical engineering he continually gave advice of a technical nature on equipment, film, printing-out papers and photo-chemicals. Until 1938 he was developing all his own film in the field. He even found time to experiment with developers and with Kodachrome film, which only became available for use in 1937.[16]

Today we remark upon the excellent technical quality of the FSA photographs, but this was not achieved without a lot of trial and error and heartaches over malfunctioning equipment and ruined film. Lee's seemingly effortless photographs which so clearly capture the essence of the rural people he visited were the result of immense effort on his part. He mastered the still awkward techniques of flashgun photography for interiors and processed his own film in hotel bathrooms at night. He carried into the field as many as seven cameras (together with lenses, tripods, light meters, flashguns, etc.), the cameras ranging in size from two 35mms with different lenses to the incredibly bulky 8 × 10 view camera.

At one point when Lee was considering adding yet another item to his repertoire—a 4 × 5 camera (which he ultimately purchased), Stryker advised against it:

Russell, it is going to be a hard winter and you save some of your money and do not go and buy a 4 × 5 yet. I am still not convinced that the 4 × 5 is as good as the 8 × 10 contact, probably it is, but you wait until we are sure of this. . . . Don't you think you might get too many cameras to work with . . . you will get dizzy trying to decide which one you want to use.[17]

Although Stryker was sympathetic to Lee's equipment problems, he did not hesitate to request that certain types of images be taken with one size camera rather than another, in spite of the inconvenience it might cause: "I believe that when you take buildings it would be well to use the 8 × 10. I realize that you can't use the big camera on everything or you will be very much slowed up in your work."[18]

Lee's technical and logistical problems in the field were compounded by the heavy and intense work schedule—weeks and months on end of constant travelling and shooting throughout the midwest and western states, every night in a hotel or tourist cabin, and day after day restaurant meals. The source of this hectic schedule was primarily Stryker's impatience to get the job done, given the uncertainties of Washington politics and patronage. He wrote to Lee in October 1937:

I don't want you to think that we are hurrying you too much. But I know that you and I share an urge alike, that is, a desire to photograph the whole United States at once. I have a feeling that if we don't do it this year, it may blow away by next year. I must come to the realization that we haven't the staff to keep up with my ambitions. You photographers will have to learn to kick back occasionally.[19]

But Lee did not kick back. He enthusiastically followed this schedule, as Stryker noted in retrospect: "Russ seemed to be able to stay on the road forever."[20] However, it is not surprising that two years of constant travel had its toll on Lee. At one point he developed severe eye strain, no doubt from too many days of constant shooting; later he had a serious throat infection which put him out of commission for many weeks.

There were other problems in these first two years that added both to the frustrations and to the excitement and challenge of the job. In May 1937, Lee's photograph of the young daughter of an Iowa farm worker sitting on her bed holding her baby brother in her arms appeared in a center spread of the *Des Moines Register* with the caption: "TENANT MADONNA. The sad expression on this young mother's face tells the whole tragic story of tenancy—low income, lack of decent housing, lack of proper food, lack of clothing and furniture." Lee's original caption had simply said "Daughter of John Scott, hired man near Ringgold County, Iowa," but the FSA copywriters without telling Lee or Stryker spiced it up with the "Tenant Madonna" line and sent it out to the newspapers, causing quite an uproar. When John Scott and his family and friends saw the spread they were not at all pleased with the condescending and inaccurate way Scott's daughter Marie had been represented. Other newspapers from Chicago to Oklahoma and Texas picked up the story and used it as a vehicle to attack the FSA, then still the Resettlement Administration. The *Daily Oklahoman* even ran the picture with a caption purportedly quoting Scott's Ringgold County neighbors: "Hell, that ain't no Madonna. That's Marie." Their article was headlined: "Iowa's Tenant Madonna Helps Out, Anyhow. She Resettles Some of the Press Agents," and with biting humor its author launched into the Resettlement Administration's "press agents," i.e., Russell Lee.

The result of this was a brouhaha almost equal to that caused by Arthur Rothstein's famous image of the steer skull photographed on the alkali flats of North Dakota. "The Skull" was attacked as a fake by local interests and caused a great deal of trouble for the Resettlement Administration.[21] Roy Stryker of course was furious about the "Tenant Madonna" incident and took appropriate steps to ameliorate the situation, but in a letter to Lee of June 21, he managed to maintain his sense of humor:

We are sending you some carbons of letters which have gone out. Those letters are an attempt to clear up your reputation in Ringgold County. It is very unfortunate this thing had to happen, but when some of the copywriters get going around this place, there seems to be no limit as to what they say. That is what happened when we got into the mess over the skull. . . . Mr Mercey has a penchant for what he calls nice "catch lines". In this case it was a catch line all right and you caught hell for it. . . . Incidently, I might add that the word "madonna" is not to be used in this office from now on, except on the chance of death. . . . I believe with all the correspondence, we can clear you sufficiently that you can venture into the County without a bullet-proof vest.[22]

Thanks to Lee's exceptionally amiable personality and his ability to relate easily to all kinds of people, incidents such as this were rare and in each new situation he readily put people at their ease, thereby creating an atmosphere conducive to the excellent documentary photography for which he is so justly praised. Roy Stryker was well aware of Lee's abilities with people. On one of his first trips into the field with Lee, recorded by F. Jack Hurley,[23] he watched in admiration as Lee approached a reluctant subject and convinced her that his work would make people aware of her plight and that she would not be demeaned by the photographs.

The seemingly effortless pictures Lee made for the FSA in the late 1930s are full of his technical skill and his exceptional visual sensitivity. Lee responded to the patterns of tires hung on the wall of a roadside garage, the arrangement of hinges on the cabinets of a sparkling kitchen, the counterpoint of textures in a rural interior. He dared to compose a couple seated symmetrically around their cabinet radio set, or to join a square dance in Pie Town, New Mexico, just because the name of the town caught his attention. With flashgun attached to his camera he mastered the lighting of his interior photographs with a success few of his colleagues could claim and was able to delineate the varying degrees of sober attention recorded on the faces of the participants in a town meeting or a church service. Stryker observed, of one of Lee's photographs of the gnarled hands of an old woman: "Russell took that with every degree of commiseration and respect. He wanted to say 'These are the hands of labor,' and he said it eloquently."[24]

Stryker's admiration for Lee's work in these first two years is well summed up in a late 1937 letter to Lee. Photographer Arthur Rothstein was considering taking another job and would need to be replaced if he did. Stryker wrote:

Do you have any suggestions for a photographer who might be interested in a job for $2600. I need not go into the qualifications, you know them. It is needless to ask you to get me another Russell Lee, because there are no such persons. I wish to God, however, that I could get another like you, but I know that is out of the question.[25]

In these first two years Lee usually travelled by himself. He and Doris had amicably separated and in 1938 were divorced. In his travels he met journalist Jean Smith in New Orleans, and they were soon married. After a honeymoon in Mexico, during which Lee took no photographs, but absorbed much appreciation for Mexican culture, Jean became an active partner in his work for the FSA, writing captions and generally assisting with the flow of work. This period became a very happy and productive one for Russell Lee. In 1939, he devoted much time and effort to photographing all over the state of Texas and produced, among other outstanding images, his in-depth series on St. Augustine, later featured in an issue of *Travel* magazine.[26]

At this time Lee, often accompanied by Jean, began to take brief trips into New Mexico. Stryker's initial instructions for what he should shoot there were as usual specific and to the point:

We are certainly looking forward to seeing the pictures which you are getting in the upper Rio Grande valley and in and around Taos. Don't forget a good ranch to go along with some of the more impoverished and small subsistence ranches. A few pictorial shots, please, such as: a row of Lombardy poplar trees with clouds in the background; shots of juniper and other trees, flowers in the background. Don't forget the picture of sagebrush you were going to get for me; a sheepherder and sheep on a hill, silhouetted against the sky; don't forget that the burro is an important part of that agriculture—we could stand quite a few shots of the little animal, taken in various poses and in various types of work in which he helps; a few pictures of the adobe churches. . . .[27]

By early 1940 Stryker was ready for a more thorough documentation of the far Southwest, which to date had only been lightly touched upon by Lee, Arthur Rothstein, and Dorothea Lange. In March 1940, as Lee was finishing up his extensive documentation of Texas, Stryker suggested that before starting to shoot in New Mexico, he take a break and do an outline of his approach to the Southwest. This outline would cover the physical characteristics of the country, agricultural patterns, major industries, population distribution, transportation, history, and problem areas.[28]

Lee sat down in Albuquerque for a few days and worked up his outline which concluded with a rating of the importance of the states for their purposes. New Mexico he rated first (above Utah, Colorado, Arizona and Nevada) and suggested allotting two months time to it. Stryker thought the idea of rating states as "excellent," and he agreed that New Mexico was number one in importance, primarily because of the multi-cultural situation there and the aridity and other problems faced by the Hispanic rural population.

A high priority for Lee's work in New Mexico was to be the "Spanish-American story," for both Stryker and Lee realized how little the Hispanic culture was known among Americans at large, yet they knew from Lee's earlier trips how fascinating were many of its aspects. Lee had reported to Stryker after his trip to Taos in September 1939 that he had been successful in getting

pictures of the life around a Spanish-American home—mostly the duties of a house wife—from feeding the rabbits, gathering vegetables in the garden, making soap at home, preparing tortillas, chile peppers and the like. Yesterday we went to another place where the Grandmother (age 75) went through all the motions of baking bread in an outdoor oven. . . . Also got pix of their house—inside and out—it was one of the neatest I have been in. The people are really grand around here—but I sure wish I had a knowledge of Spanish.[29]

Early in April 1940, Stryker suggested to Lee that he make contact with Dr. George Sanchez, a native-born sociologist, since known for his pioneering work on Hispanic New Mexicans. Stryker had been visited by Al Hurt of the Amarillo Land Coordinator's Office. Hurt brought him "the manuscript of Sanchez' new book on the Spanish-Americans. He says it is the finest thing that has ever been done. . . ." Stryker told Lee to try to find Sanchez in Albuquerque and "tell him that you . . . would like to have a chance to see the manuscript and talk with him about the whole Spanish-American situation."[30]

Lee's meeting with George Sanchez proved to be very productive, for through Sanchez he was able to gain a real understanding of the rural Hispanic culture of northern New Mexico. Lee was impressed with Sanchez' grasp of the situation and wrote to Stryker: "He certainly knows the problems of the Spanish Americans." Stryker suggested to Lee that "concentrated work in *one* of the isolated Spanish-American villages would be very representative of them all."[31]

By June, thanks to Sanchez' advice, Lee had determined that the Taos County communities of Chamisal and Peñasco would be ideal for an in-depth documentation of Spanish-American culture. "These towns and this district were recommended by Dr. Sanchez and also by Dr. [Eshrev] Shevky who has done a great deal of intelligent work in the Spanish-American villages." These isolated mountain villages had the added appeal of being virgin territory for the documentary photographer. As Lee wrote to Stryker, "these towns have not been covered by the SCS [Soil Conservation Service] in their photographic work."[32]

In late June of 1940 the Lees left Albuquerque for Taos County, setting up headquarters in the town of Dixon and beginning to make contacts for work in Chamisal and Peñasco. In July Lee wrote Stryker that he had been

terribly busy getting the ground work laid at Peñasco and Chamisal—the 2 S.A. [Spanish-American] towns I'm taking pictures of. Have taken quite a few already, but it has been rather slow work because of having had to talk to so many people. . . . I believe I'll be able to get many phases of this S.A. life that have not been generally pictured. On Tuesday morning I am moving to Peñasco to stay with a private family and we will probably take our meals there too. Have met the priest, postmaster, mayordomo, merchants and several of the farmers and should have a pretty good story on Peñasco & Chamisal by the end of next week. . . .[33]

This shows the thoroughness with which Lee prepared the groundwork in Peñasco and Chamisal for his "Spanish-American story" and his sense of its importance. The present publication shows the fruits of his work there, a remarkable visual document of Hispanic village life at the end of the 1930s.

The Spanish-American story was of such importance and Lee's work in Chamisal and

Peñasco so outstanding that Stryker hoped to do a picture book about it, combining Lee's photographs with an interpretive text by an expert in the field, in order to get the little-known material before the general public. In September 1940 Lee suggested to Stryker that he "contact Al Hurt as regards a prospective author for the Spanish-American book, or George Sanchez might even be interested in working on it. He has one book projected, I believe, but the picture book might act as a fill in for his other study. . . . Dr. Shevky of SCS at Albuquerque knows the area extremely well—his subordinate— Ernest Maes—knows the Spanish-American area even better. Incidently, I would suggest that you try to find someone who is Spanish-American to write that book."[34] In spite of his initial enthusiasm about Sanchez' work, Stryker did not consider him a suitable author for the book:

I am looking for someone to do the text to accompany the pictures on the Spanish-American towns. We will have to watch carefully that we may find some one who has literary ability. I doubt very much if Sanchez could do the book; he knows his material, but his writing is pretty academic.[35]

Unfortunately, with the nation's attention turned increasingly to war, the project for a book on the Hispanic towns was shelved—just at the historical moment that the towns themselves experienced the jarring loss of the traditions recorded by Lee and the modernization brought about by the onset of that war.

A little more than a year later, America too was at war. Lee was recruited by Pare Lorentz to join a unit devoted to the recording of aerial navigation routes. He distinguished himself by producing many thousands of photographs that were an essential component of the briefing of pilots bound for unfamiliar bases all over the world. Highly commended and with the rank of major, Lee left the service exhausted and looking forward to a long vacation. But early in 1946, on a strong recommendation from Lorentz, Lee was summoned back to Washington to provide documentation for a Department of Interior study of conditions in America's coal mines. His photographs from Harlan County, Kentucky, once again anticipated preoccupations given broad public attention three decades later. The exceptional effectiveness of his recording was instrumental in bringing about the first serious attempt to regulate working conditions in the mines, and demonstrated the remarkable professionalism and sensitivity Lee brought to his work.

The postwar years brought Lee a steady series of important assignments. He was part of a Standard Oil photographic team headed by Roy Stryker. He undertook freelance assignments for magazines. In 1965 he began to teach at the University of Texas in Austin, where he and his wife Jean had made their home since 1947. The versatility of his work, the technical skill he seemed to have so naturally, and the ease with which he could relate to people he wished to photograph have inspired a generation of students and colleagues with whom he has worked.

Clearly, Lee's career has been a varied and successful one. Yet, when he reflected on it in 1964, he observed that his work for the FSA "was the best job I ever had . . . it was wonderful in the scope, and I was my own boss, more or less, and I just kept as busy as the devil . . . I'd never worked so hard in my life."[36]

The strength of his personality has prevented Lee from falling victim to stereotypes. Even in his work in the most depressed areas of the country (or the world) his photographs do not overstress the hopelessness of his subjects. Indeed, he often depicts them leading comparatively serene and dignified lives, although the evidence shows that they should be reduced to abject misery. Far from it! Lee has seen that people of character work willingly, relax in the evening, take pride in their children, and delight in whatever touches of graciousness they can have around them. His directness of vision, ability to capture the telling moment, and sense of humor endow his photographs with a unique power.

As he looked back on the accomplishments of the FSA Roy Stryker wrote: "We succeeded in doing exactly what Rex Tugwell said we should do: *We introduced Americans to America*. . . . The full effect of this . . . work was that it helped connect one generation's image of itself with the reality of its own time in history."[37] It is satisfying to realize that a government project involving a dozen people with uncommon vision and dedication should be so carefully studied today, forty years after its close. And it is splendid that Russell Lee can be around to see his photographs with a new audience and inform a new generation.

Pare Lorentz has said: "I would characterize Russell Lee as a craftsman, as being comparable to the old-time tramp printers . . .; they could walk into a newspaper shop and do anything from set type to writing poetry to reporting the lead news story. I can best describe Russ Lee, as a person, by the two sounds he frequently makes. One he makes when you first propose a course of action to him. It is a sort of 'umh-Humh!' . . . That's a contemplative sound. The other, and more frequent, is simply: 'Well, fine, fine— mighty fine.' "[38] Anyone who has met Russell Lee will smile at the accuracy of this characterization. As he approaches eighty Lee no longer heads off the main road to Pie Town or Chamisal so readily, but he remains the alert, deeply caring, talented individual who first picked up a camera almost half a century ago.

NOTES

1. Roy E. Stryker and Nancy Wood, *In This Proud Land* (Greenwich: New York Graphic Society, 1973), p. 7. In *Roy Stryker: The Humane Propagandist* (Louisville, 1977), Calvin Kytle states that he actually wrote this essay for Stryker. Although Riis's photographic work did not receive critical acclaim until the 1940s, his books—*How the Other Half Lives* (1890), *Children of the Poor* (1892), and *The Making of an American* (1901)—are illustrated with his documentary photographs of slum conditions, and the latter two describe in detail his methods and experiences in documentary photography. These volumes went through numerous editions during the early 1900s and were readily available to socially-concerned people such as Tugwell and Stryker.

2. F. Jack Hurley, *Portrait of a Decade: Roy Stryker and the Development of Documentary Photography in the Thirties* (Baton Rouge: Louisiana State University Press, 1972), pp. 26–27.

3. Ibid., p. 36.

4. Stryker and Wood, *Proud Land*, p. 7.

5. Ibid.

6. Russell Lee, interview with Richard K. Doud for the Archives of American Art, 2 June 1964, p. 3. The excerpts quoted here are from the unedited transcript in the Archives and are cited with permission of the Archives and Russell Lee.

7. Ibid., p. 21.

8. Stryker to Lee, 19 January 1937, Roy Stryker Papers, University of Louisville. Unless otherwise noted, all references below to correspondence are from documents in this University of Louisville collection.

9. Lee to Stryker, 22 January 1937.

10. Stryker to Lee, 10 April 1937.

11. Stryker to Lee, 24 June 1937.

12. Stryker to Lee, 27 March 1940. Stryker apparently did not recognize any difference between Weston's "straight" photography and the more sentimental work of the pictorialists.

13. Stryker to Lee, 19 January 1937, and 30 October 1937.

14. Lee to Stryker, Mt. Ayr, Iowa, 24 December 1936.

15. Lee to Edwin Locke (Stryker's administrative assistant), 15 September 1937.

16. Beaumont Newhall, *The History of Photography* (New York: Museum of Modern Art, 1982), p. 276.

17. Stryker to Lee, 12 October 1937.

18. Stryker to Lee, 5 October 1937.

19. Ibid.

20. Quoted in F. Jack Hurley, *Russell Lee, Photographer* (Dobbs Ferry: Morgan and Morgan, 1978), p. 16.

21. On the controversy over Rothstein's "The Skull," see Hurley, *Portrait of a Decade*, pp. 86–92.

22. Stryker to Lee, 21 June 1937. Also see A. A. Mercey to Lee, 21 June 1937, in which Mercey acknowledges that the Division of Information was responsible for the offending "Tenant Madonna" caption and apologizes for the trouble it caused. In a later incident after the outbreak of World War II, Lee was suspected of being a German spy when he took photographs of copper mining operations in isolated Mogollon, New Mexico. He succeeded in convincing local authorities that he was legitimately working for the FSA, but the incident caused quite a stir in the town.

23. Hurley, *Russell Lee*, p. 18.

24. Stryker and Wood, *Proud Land*, p. 7.

25. Stryker to Lee, 1 November 1937.

26. Mark Adams and Russell Lee, "Our Town in East Texas," *Travel*, March 1940, pp. 5–12. When Stryker first saw Lee's St. Augustine images as they emerged from the developing trays in the lab, he wrote: "You certainly did go to town in that place! I am very anxious to get them in my hands so I can go over them rather carefully" (Stryker to Lee, 17 May 1939).

27. Stryker to Lee, September 1939.

28. Stryker to Lee, 19 March 1940.

29. Lee to Stryker, September 1939.

30. Stryker to Lee, 4 April 1940.

31. Lee to Stryker, 20 April 1940.

32. Lee to Stryker, 24 June 1940. It is interesting to note that Lee was singularly unimpressed when he met Soil Conservation Service photographer Irving Rusinow, whose *A Camera Report on El Cerrito: A Typical Spanish-American Community in New Mexico* (USDA, Bureau of Agricultural Economics, Government Printing Office, 1942) is the only previously published photographic survey of Hispanic village life at the time. After meeting Rusinow in Mexico in January 1940, Lee wrote: "He is the photographer from Albuquerque who did some work for SCS. He was trying to get a job with the Mexican government to do some work among the people both industrial and agricultural . . . but he is up against a real handicap—he doesn't know the language and

seemed to know little about the people'' (Lee to Stryker, January 1940).

33. Lee to Stryker, 13 July 1940.

34. Lee to Stryker, 7 September 1940.

35. Stryker to Lee, 10 September 1940.

36. Lee interview with Doud, p. 20.

37. Stryker and Wood, *Proud Land*, p. 9.

38. *Russell Lee: Retrospective Exhibition, 1934–64* (Austin: The University Art Museum of the University of Texas, 1965), unpaginated.